FINGERPICKING
Acoustic ROCK

14 Songs Arranged for Solo Guitar in Standard Notation & Tablature

ISBN-13: 978-1-4234-0728-7

HAL•LEONARD®
CORPORATION

7777 W. BLUEMOUND RD. P.O. BOX 13819 MILWAUKEE, WI 53213

Visit Hal Leonard Online at
www.halleonard.com

Angie

Words and Music by Mick Jagger and Keith Richards

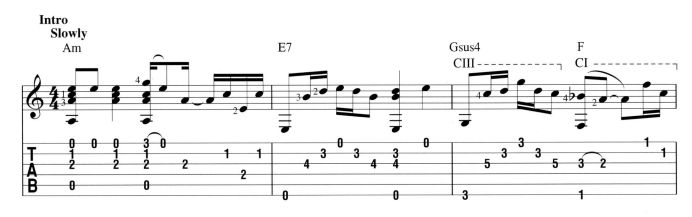

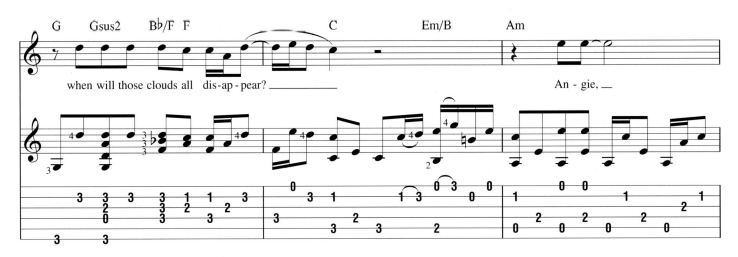

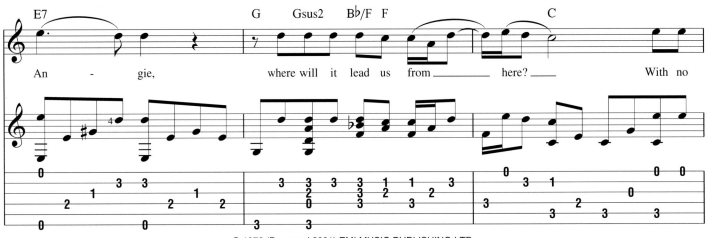

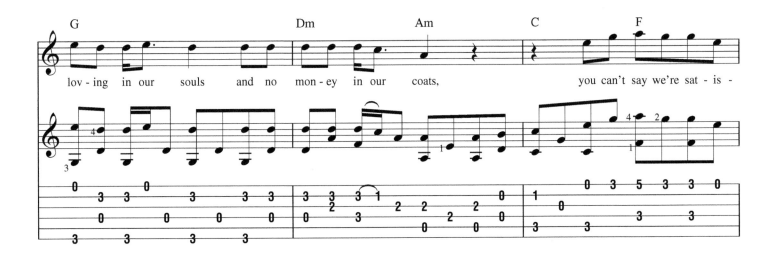

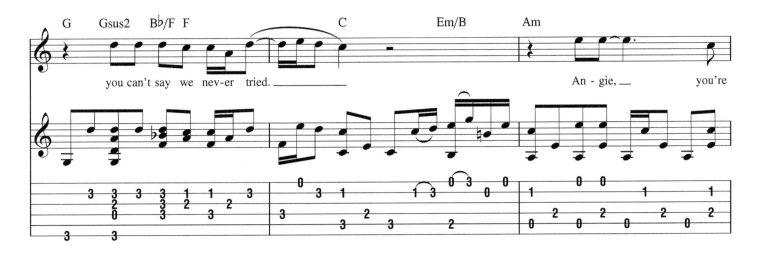

Babe, I'm Gonna Leave You

Words and Music by Anne Bredon, Jimmy Page and Robert Plant

Intro
Moderately slow

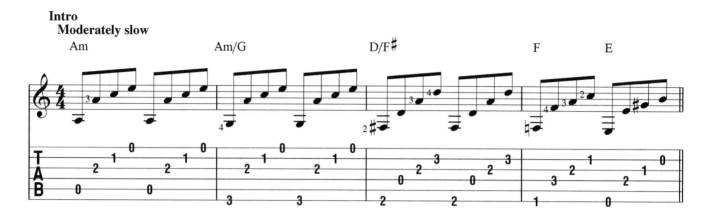

Verse

1. Babe, ba-by, ba-by, ___ I'm gon-na

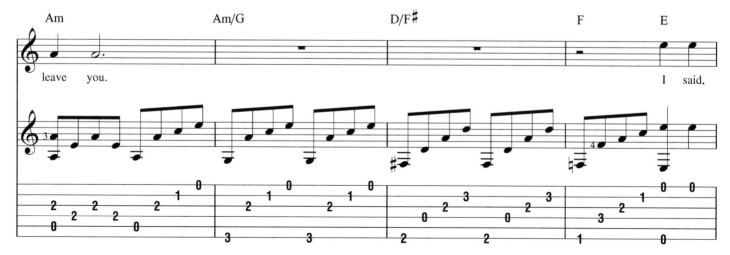

leave you. I said,

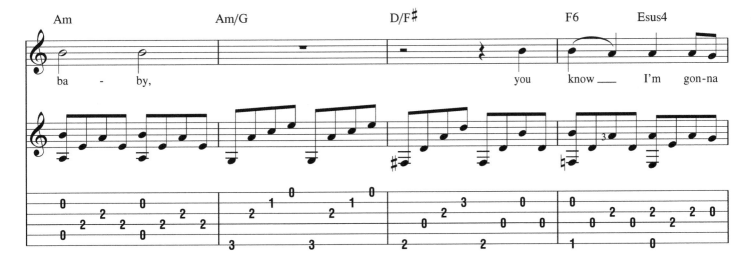

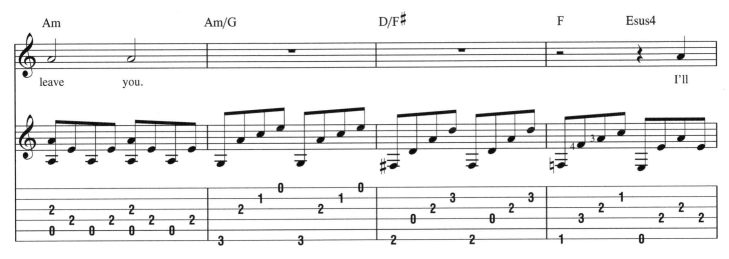

Bridge

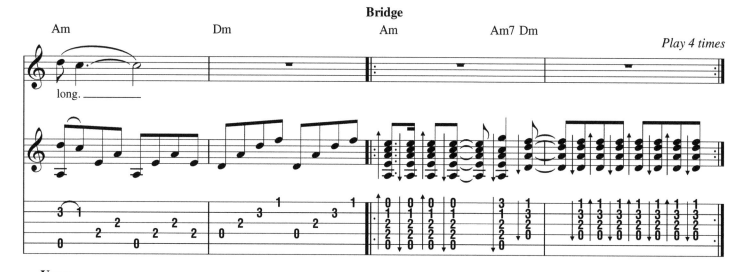

Verse

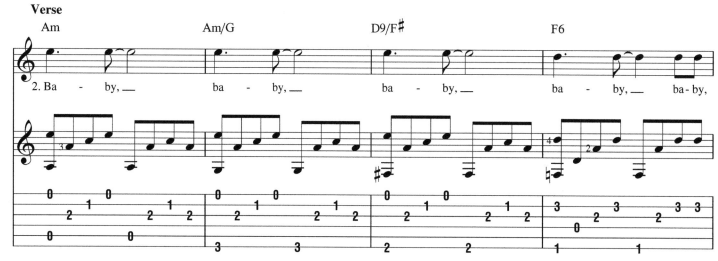

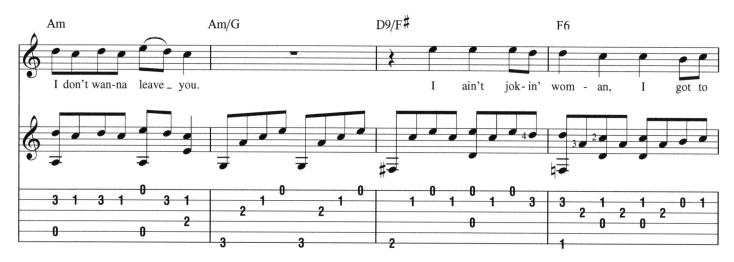

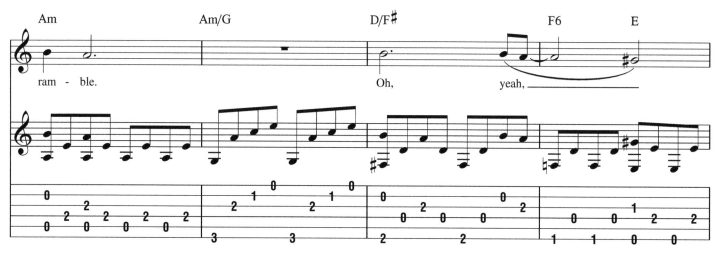

Band on the Run

Words and Music by Paul and Linda McCartney

Drop D tuning:
(low to high)D-A-D-G-B-E

Intro
Moderately slow

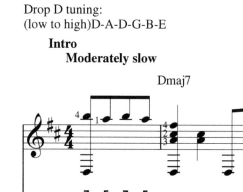
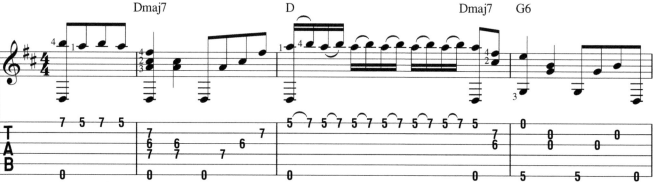

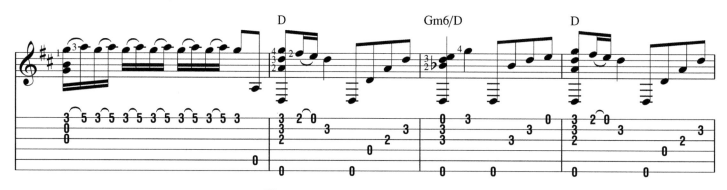

Verse

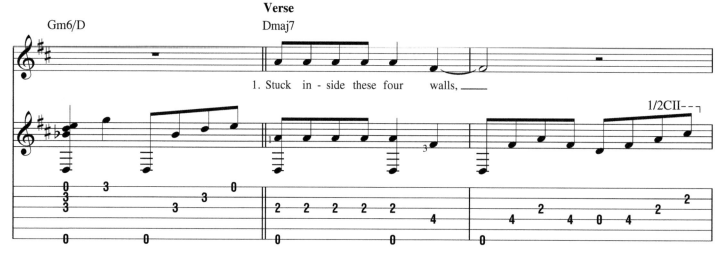

1. Stuck in - side these four   walls, _____

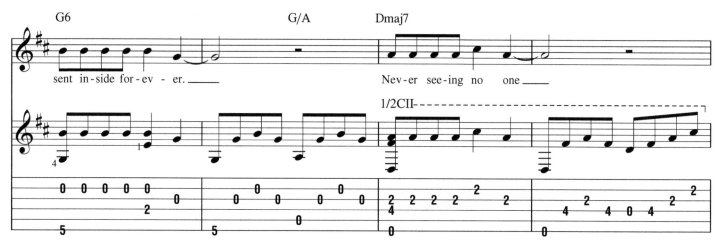

sent in-side for-ev - er. _____   Nev-er see-ing no   one _____

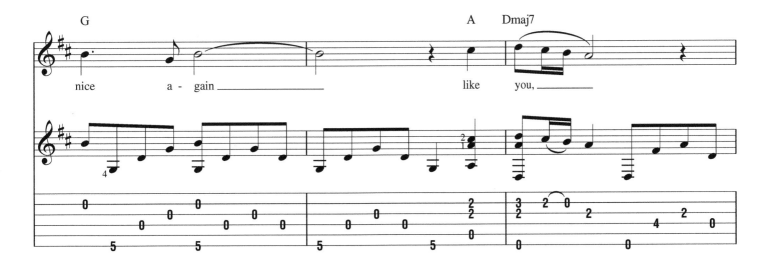

Interlude

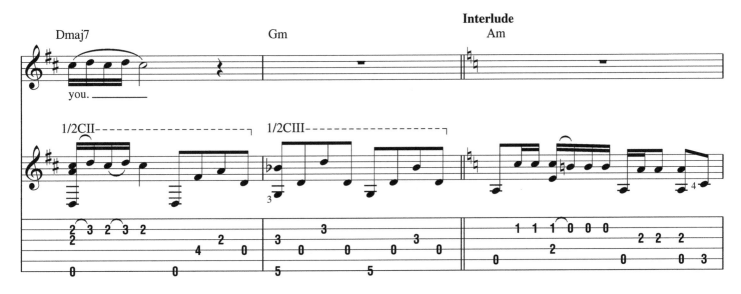

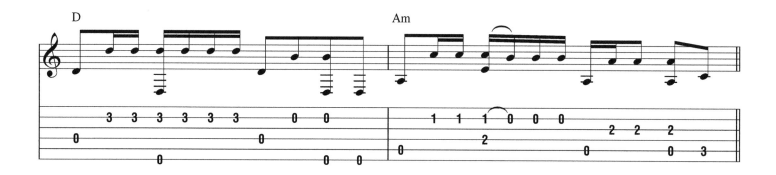

Bridge

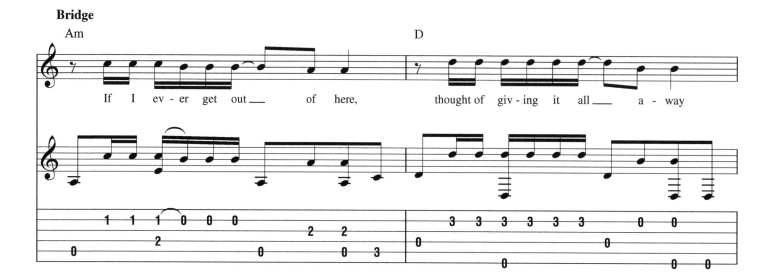

If I ev - er get out ____ of here, thought of giv - ing it all ____ a - way

to a reg - is - tered char ____ - i - ty. All I need is a pint ____ a day. If I

ev - er get out ____ of here. ____ (If we ev - er get out ____ of here.)

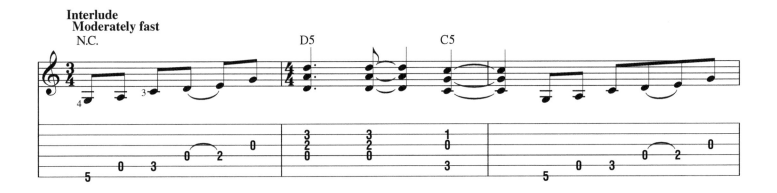

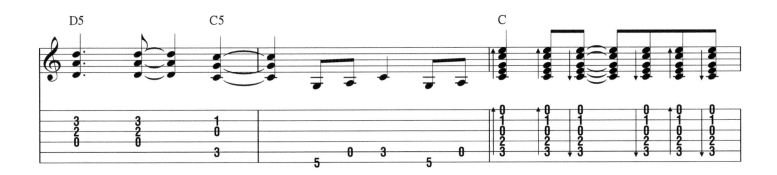

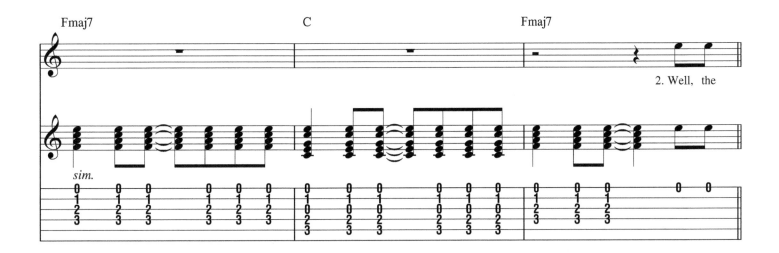

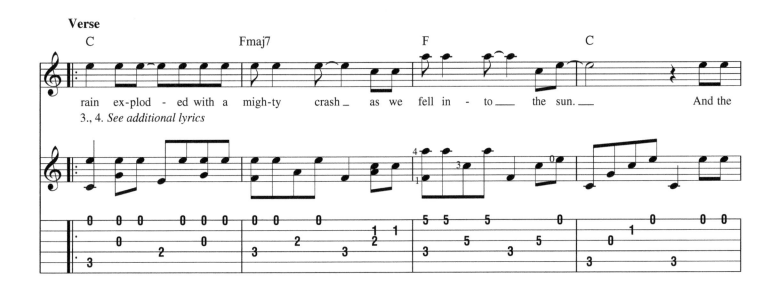

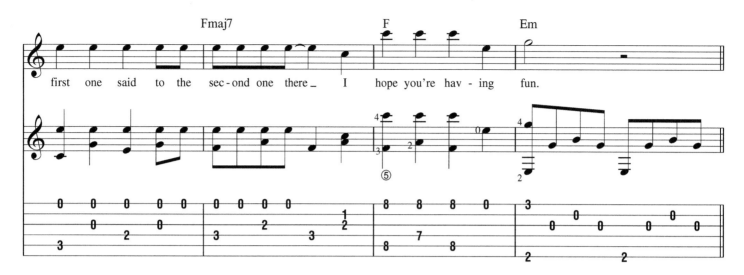

first one said to the sec-ond one there _ I hope you're hav-ing fun.

Chorus

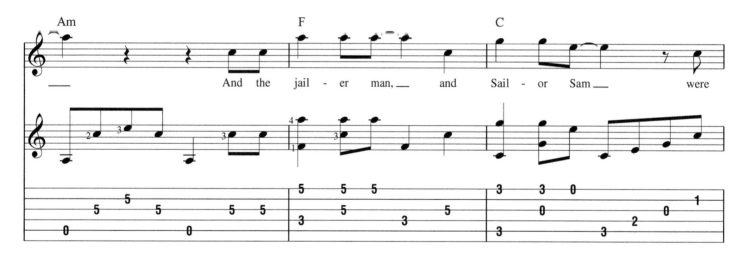

Band on the run, ___ band on the run. _

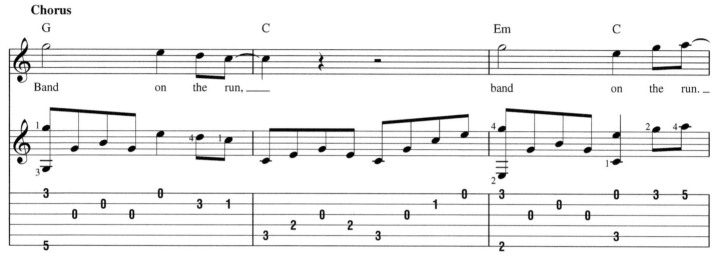

___ And the jail - er man, ___ and Sail - or Sam ___ were

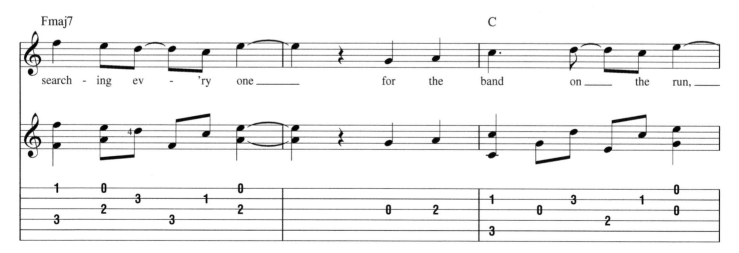

search - ing ev - 'ry one _____ for the band on ___ the run, ___

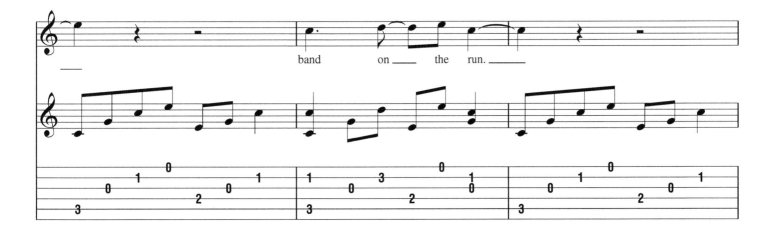

band on the run.

Band on the run, band on the run.

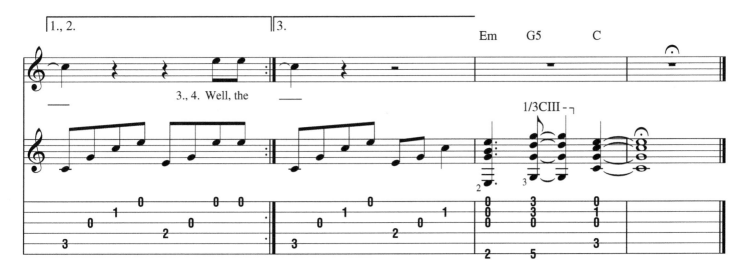

| 1., 2. | 3. | Em | G5 | C |

3., 4. Well, the

Additional Lyrics

3. Well, the undertaker drew a heavy sigh
   Seeing no one else had come.
   And a bell was ringing in the village square
   For the rabbits on the run.

4. Well, the night was falling as the desert world
   Began to settle down.
   In the town, they're searching for us ev'rywhere
   But we never will be found.

Bridge Over Troubled Water

Words and Music by Paul Simon

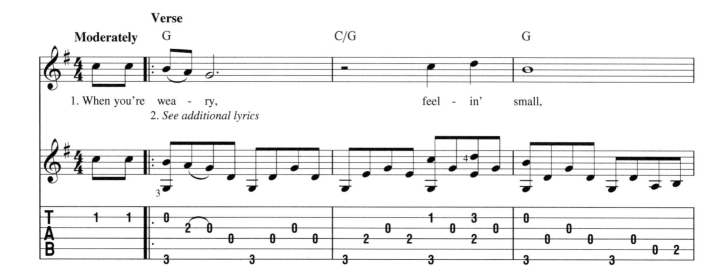

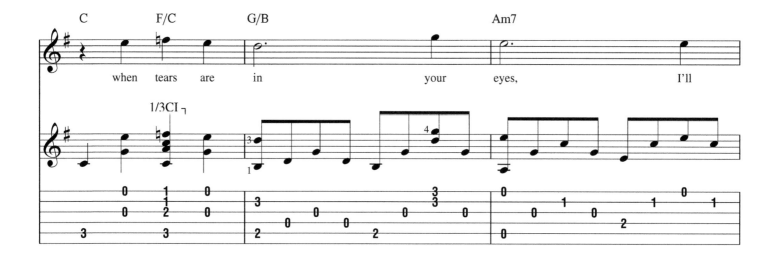

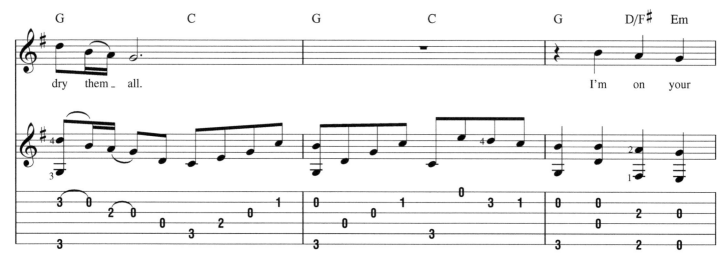

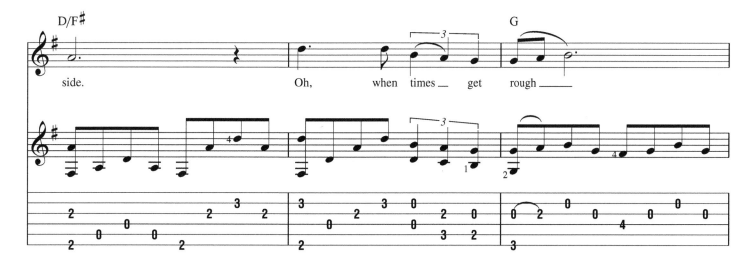

side. Oh, when times ___ get rough _____

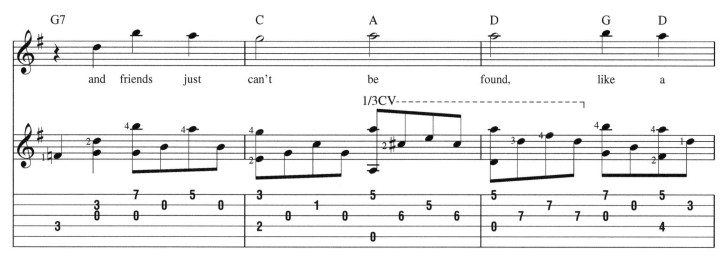

and friends just can't be found, like a

bridge o - ver trou - bled wa - ter, I will lay me

down. Like a bridge o - ver trou - bled wa - ter, I will lay me

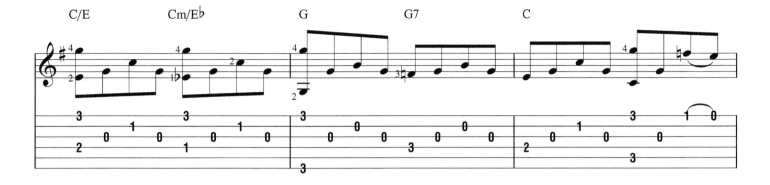

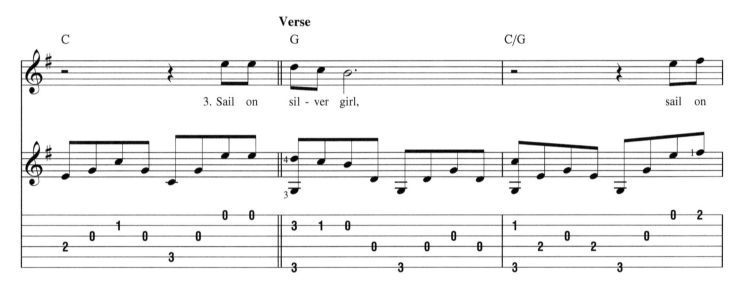

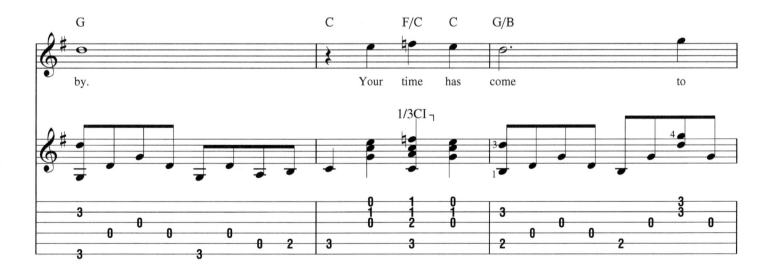

Additional Lyrics

2. When you're down and out, when you're on the street,
   When evening falls so hard, I'll comfort you.
   I'll take your part. Oh, when darkness comes and pain is all around,
   Like a bridge over troubled water, I will lay me down.
   Like a bridge over troubled water, I will lay me down.

Every Rose Has Its Thorn

**Words and Music by Bobby Dall, Brett Michaels,
Bruce Johannesson and Rikki Rockett**

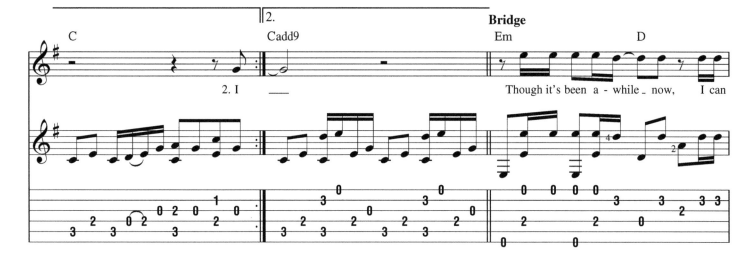

2. I _____

Bridge

Em · D

Though it's been a-while _ now, I can

still feel so much pain. _ Like the knife that cuts _ you, the wound heals, but the scar, that scar re-

Interlude

mains.

sim.

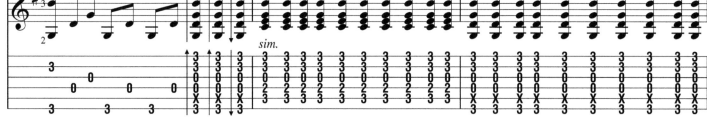

Verse

Cadd9 · G

3. I know I could have saved a love that night _ if I'd

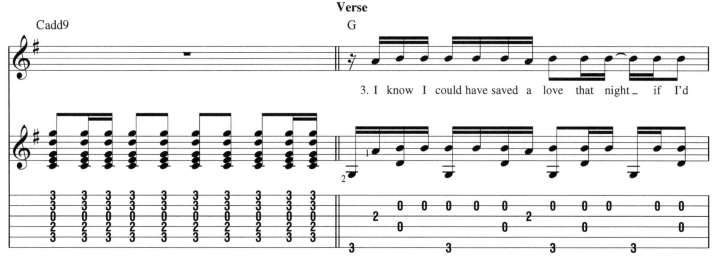

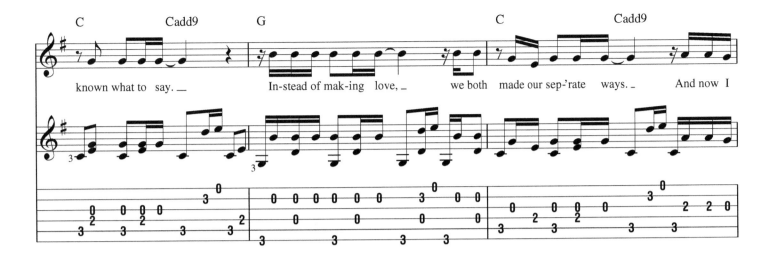

known what to say. ___   In-stead of mak-ing love, ___   we both made our sep-'rate ways. ___   And now I

hear you found some-bod-y new ___ and   that I nev-er meant that much to   you. ___   To   hear that tears me up   in - side, ___ and to

O Coda

D.S. al Coda

see   you cuts me   like   a   knife. ___   I guess

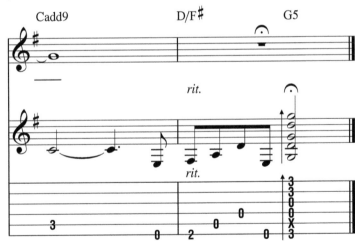

Additional Lyrics

2. I listen to our fav'rite song
   Playin' on the radio.
   Hear the D.J. say,
   "Love's a game of easy come and easy go."
   But, I wonder, does he know?
   Has he ever felt like this?
   And I know that you'd be right here now
   If I coulda let you know somehow.
   I guess...

I'd Love to Change the World

Words and Music by Alvin Lee

Intro
Moderately

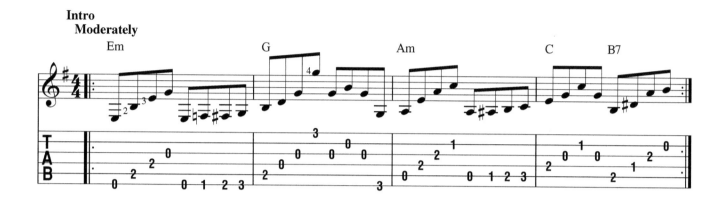

Verse

1. Ev - 'ry-where is   freaks _ and hair - ies,   dykes _ and fair - ies.
2. *See additional lyrics*

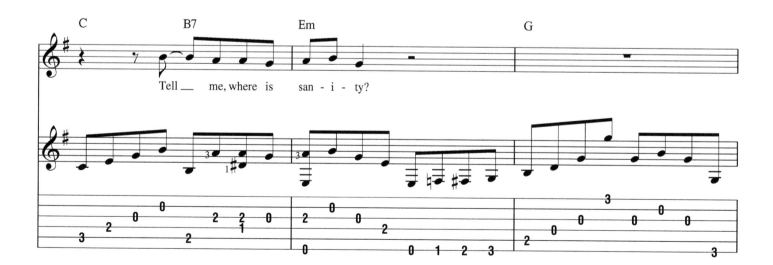

Tell _ me, where is   san - i - ty?

𝄋 Chorus

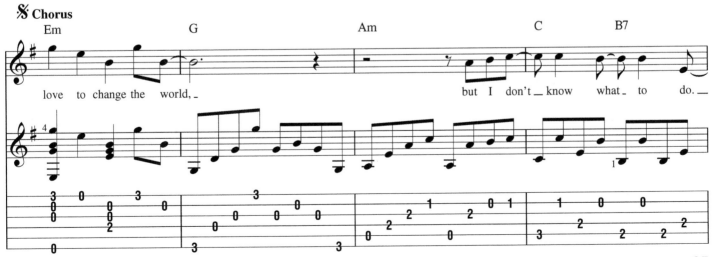

25

Additional Lyrics

2. Population keeps on breeding.
   Nation bleeding, still more feeding economy.
   Life is funny; skies are sunny.
   Bees make honey; who needs money?
   Monopoly.
   No, not for me.

Knockin' on Heaven's Door

Words and Music by Bob Dylan

Intro
Moderately

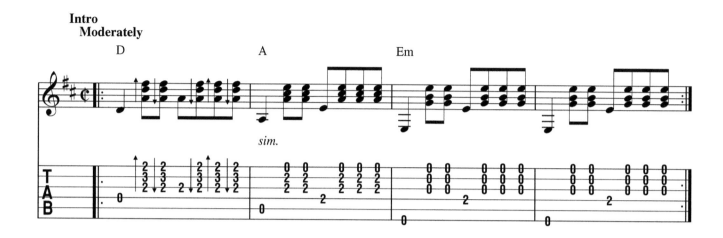

Verse

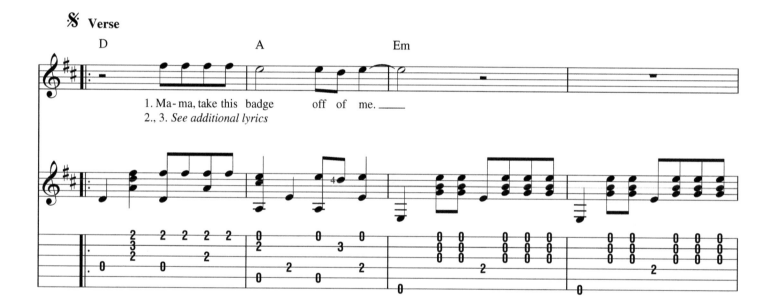

1. Ma-ma, take this badge off of me. ___
2., 3. *See additional lyrics*

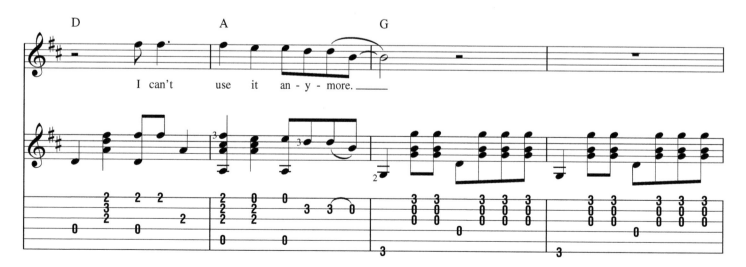

I can't use it an-y-more. ___

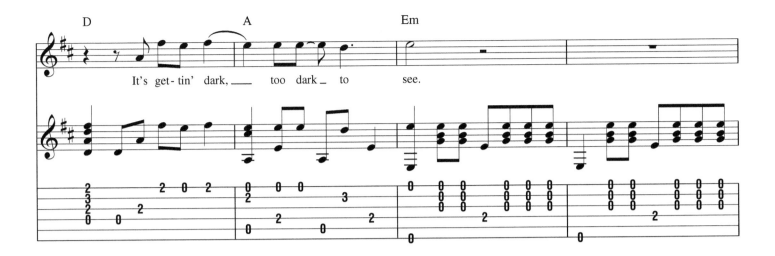

It's get-tin' dark, ___ too dark _ to see.

I feel I'm knock-in' on heav-en's door. _

Chorus

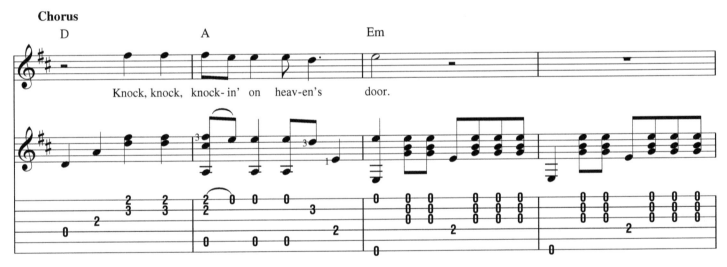

Knock, knock, knock-in' on heav-en's door.

Knock, knock, knock-in' on heav-en's door. _

Knock, knock, knock- in' on heav-en's door.

Just like so man - y times be - fore. _____

D.S. al Coda

Just like so man - y times be - fore. _____

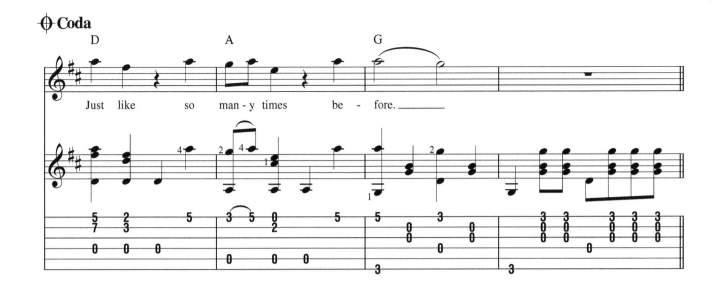

Coda

Just like so man-y times be - fore. _____

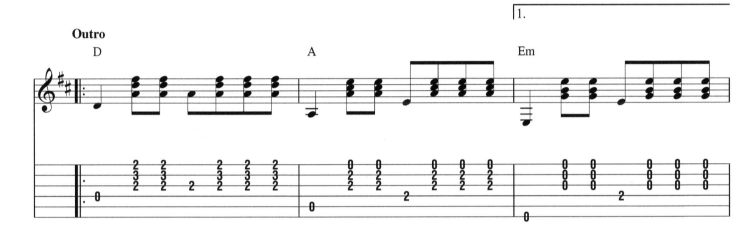

Outro

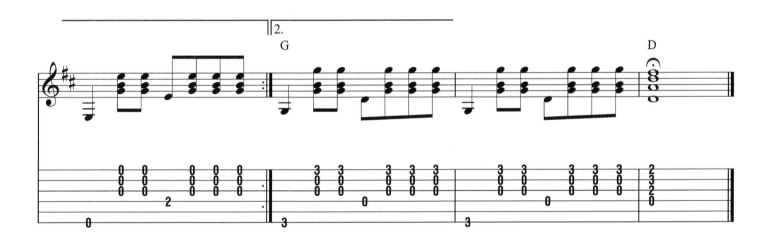

Additional Lyrics

2. Mama, wipe the blood out of my face.
   I just can't see through it anymore.
   Got a long black feelin' and it's hard to trace,
   And I feel like I'm knockin' on heaven's door.

3. Mama, lay them guns onto the ground.
   I just can't fire them anymore.
   That long black cape is pulling on down,
   And I feel like I' knockin' on heaven's door.

Landslide

Words and Music by Stevie Nicks

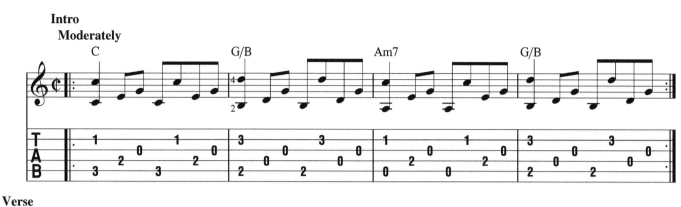

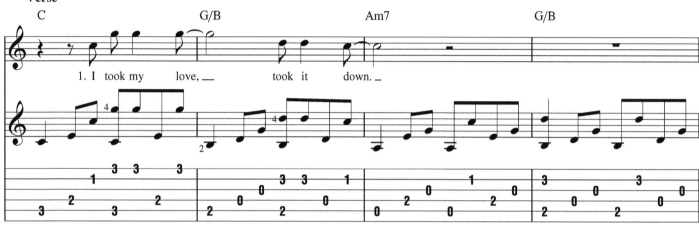

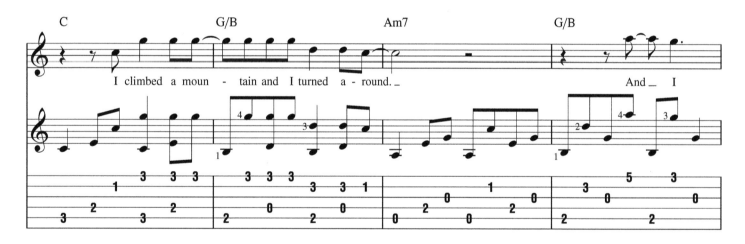

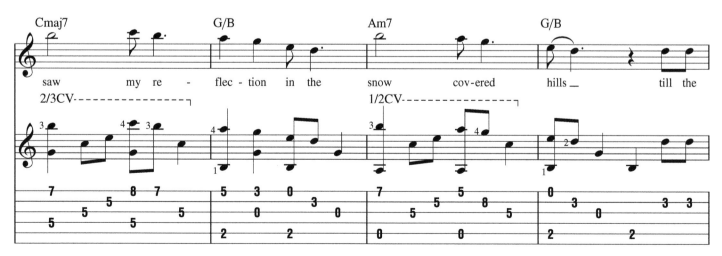

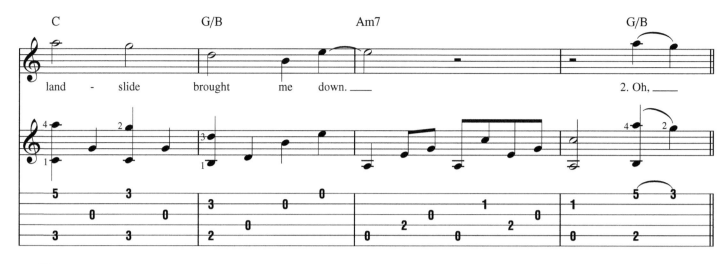

land - slide brought me down. _____ 2. Oh, _____

Verse

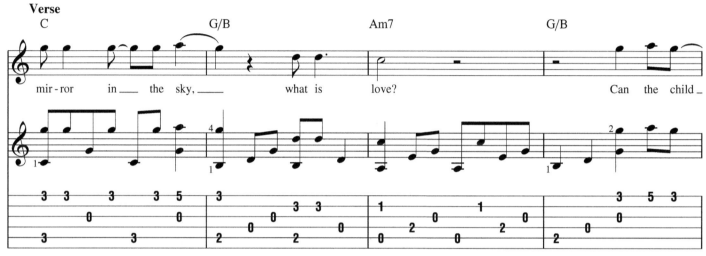

mir - ror in _____ the sky, _____ what is love? Can the child _____

_____ with - in my heart rise a - bove? Can I

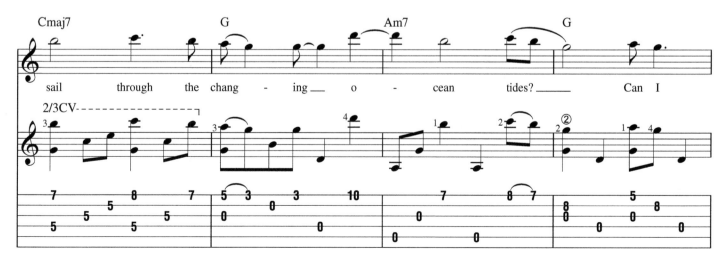

sail through the chang - ing _____ o - cean tides? _____ Can I

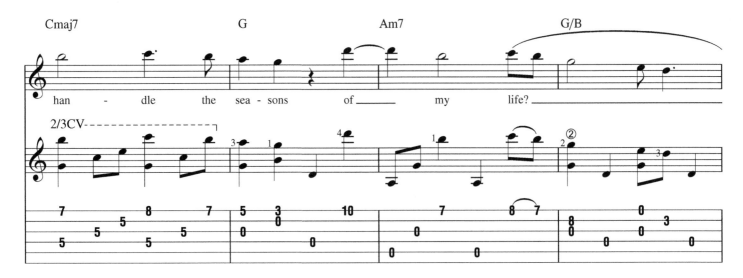

han - dle the sea - sons of _____ my life? _____

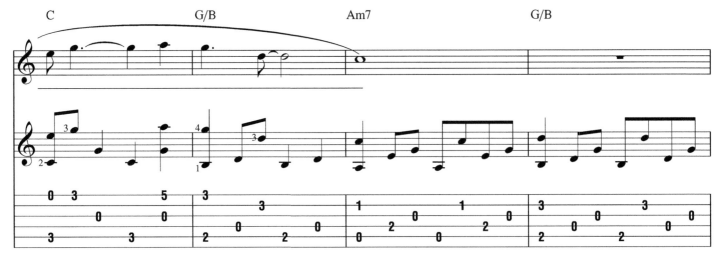

Mm. _____

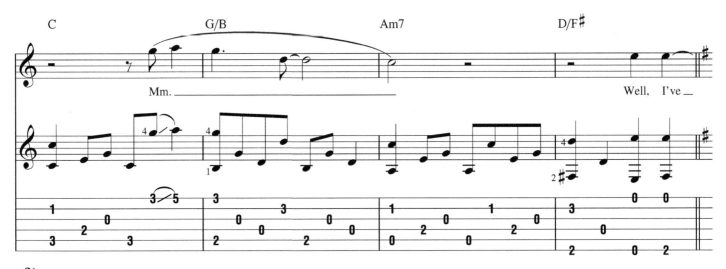

Well, I've _____

Chorus

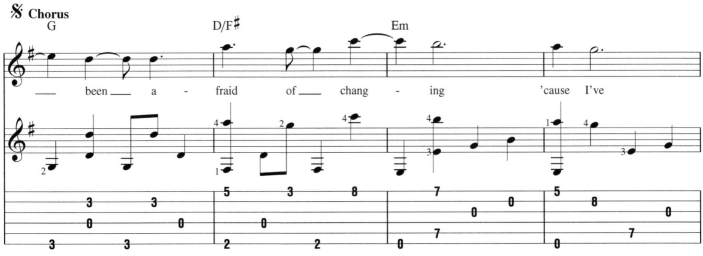

_____ been _____ a - fraid of _____ chang - ing 'cause I've

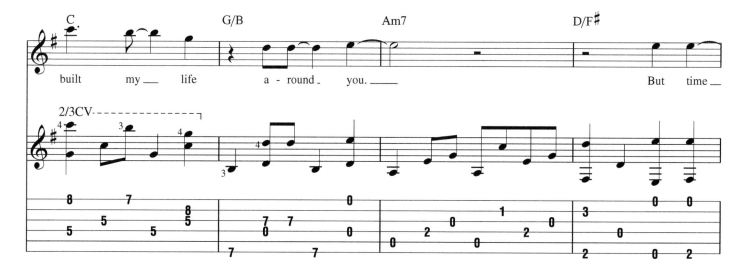

built my ___ life a - round ___ you. _____ But time ___

___ makes ___ you bold - er; e - ven child - ren ___ get old - er, ___ and

To Coda ⊕

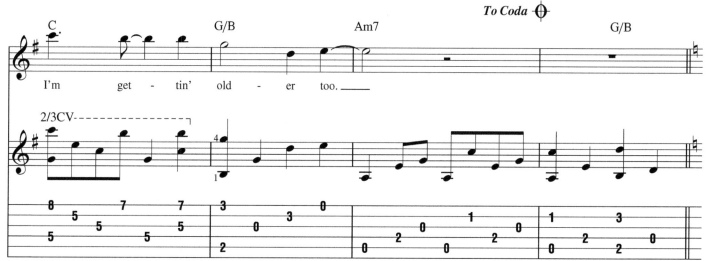

I'm get - tin' old - er too. _____

1.

Interlude

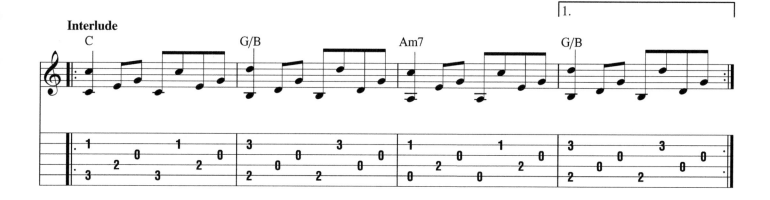

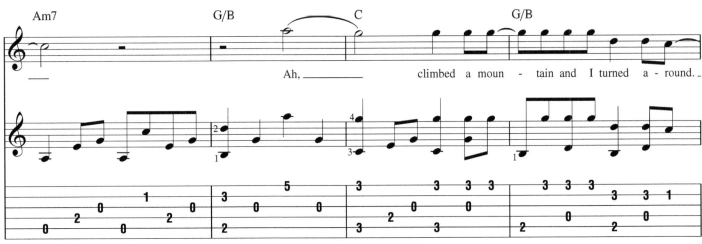

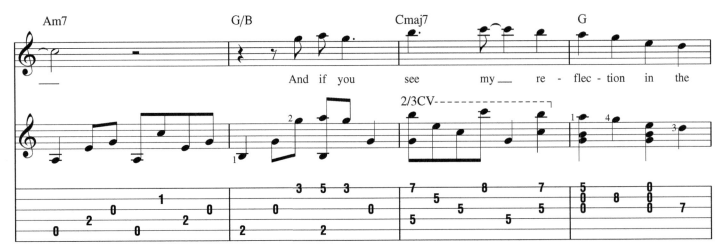

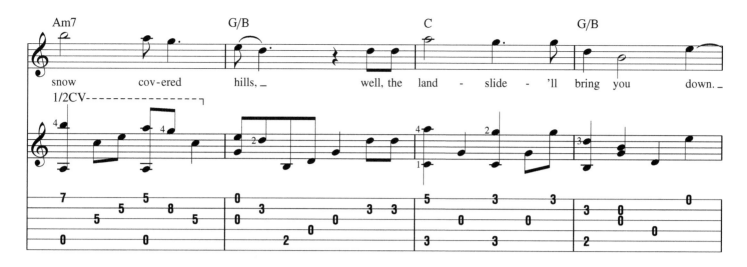

snow cov-ered hills, _ well, the land - slide - 'll bring you down. _

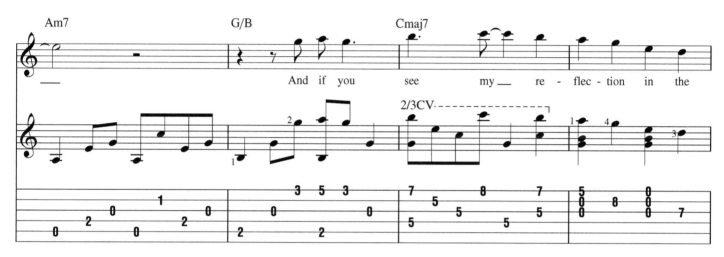

_ And if you see my _ re - flec - tion in the

snow cov - ered hills, _____ well, the land - slide - 'll bring you down. _

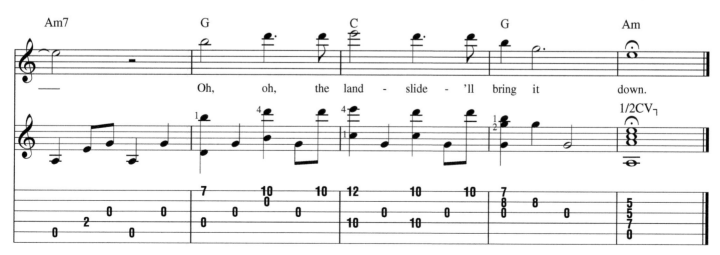

_ Oh, oh, the land - slide - 'll bring it down.

Layla

Words and Music by Eric Clapton and Jim Gordon

*Roll 3rd finger

1. What will you do when you get lone - ly?
No one wait-ing by your side.
2., 3. *See additional lyrics*

You've been run - nin', and hid - in' much too long. You know it's just your fool-ish pride. Lay - la,

got me on my knees. Lay - la, beg- gin' dar- lin', please. Lay - la,

Additional Lyrics

2. Tried to give you consolation,
   Your old man had let you down.
   Like a fool, I fell in love with you.
   You turned my whole world upside down.

3. Make the best of the situation,
   Before I fin'ly go insane.
   Please don't say we'll never find a way.
   Tell me all my love's in vain.

More Than Words

Words and Music by Nuno Bettencourt and Gary Cherone

1. Say-ing "I ___ love ___ you" is not the words ___ I want ___ to ___ hear ___ from you. ___
2. *See additional lyrics*

___ It's not that I ___ want ___ you not to say, ___ but if ___ you ___ on - ly knew ___

how ___ eas - y ___ it would be ___ to ___ show ___ me how ___ you feel. ___

Chorus

More than words _____ is all you have _ to _ do _ to make _ it _ real. _

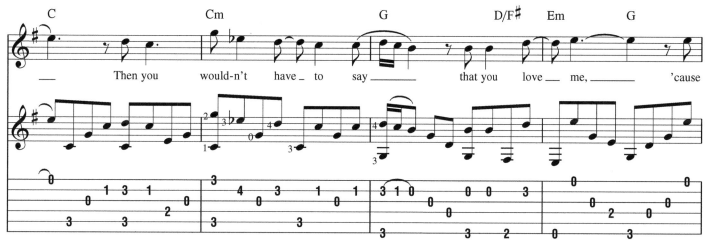

Then you would-n't have _ to say _____ that you love _ me, _____ 'cause

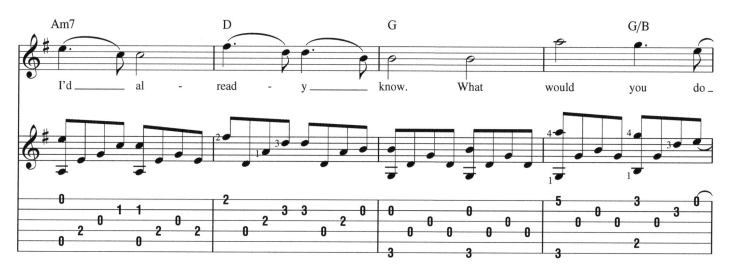

I'd _____ al - read - y _____ know. What would you do _

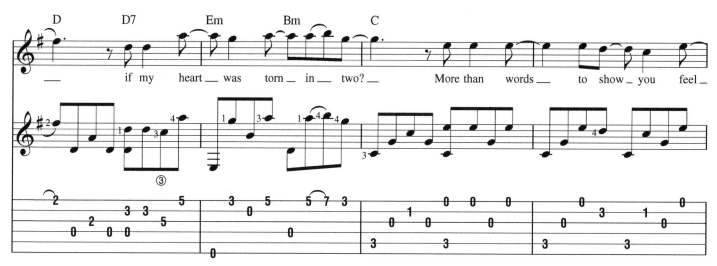

if my heart _ was torn _ in _ two? _ More than words _ to show _ you feel _

that your love __ for me __ is real. __ What would you say __

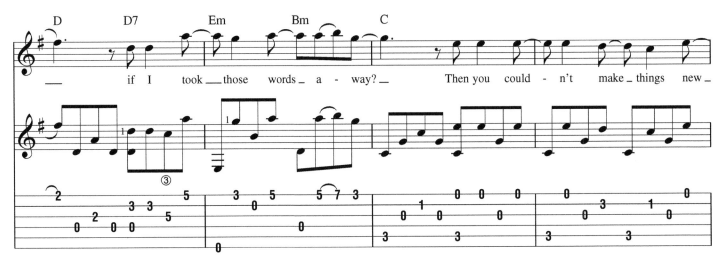

if I took __ those words __ a - way? __ Then you could - n't make __ things new __

To Coda ⊕　　　　　　　　　　**Interlude**

just by say - ing "I __ love __ you." __　　　　La, dee, da, __ la, dee, da, __

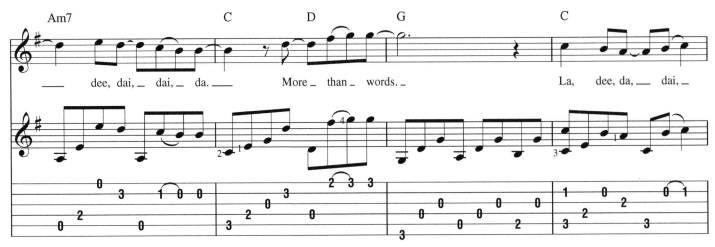

dee, dai, __ dai, __ da. __　　More __ than __ words. __　　La, dee, da, __ dai, __

42

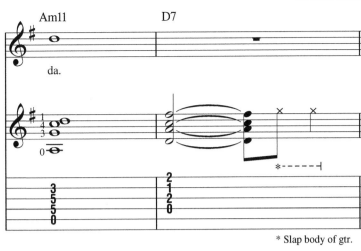

Coda

* Slap body of gtr.

Outro

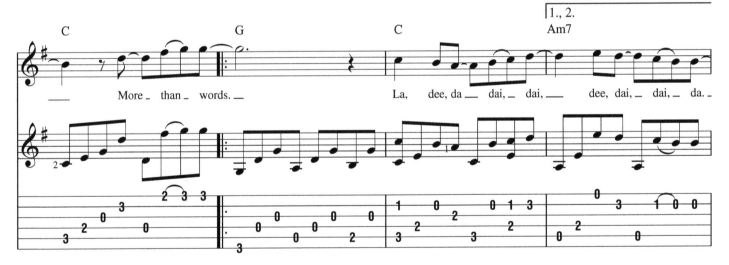

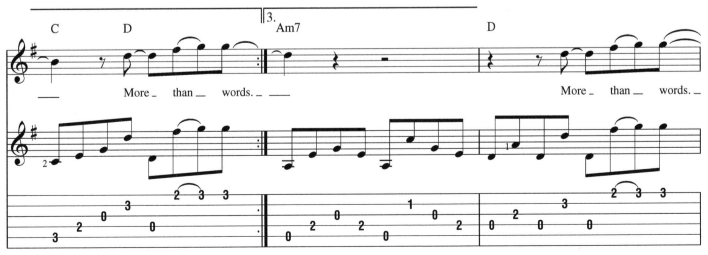

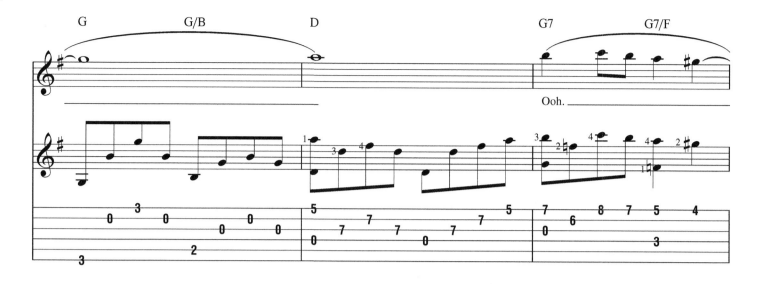

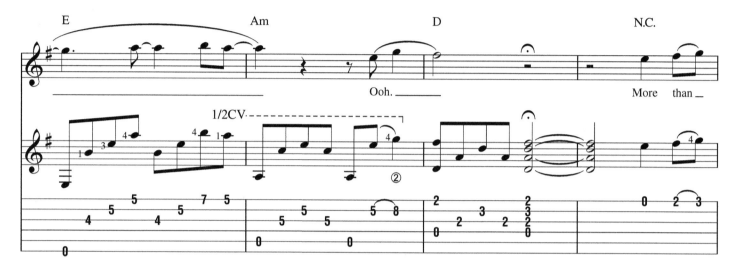

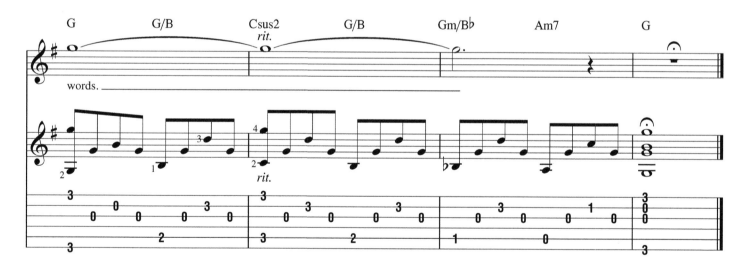

Additional Lyrics

2. Now that I've tried to talk to you
   And make you understand,
   All you have to do is close your eyes
   And just reach out your hands and touch me.
   Hold me close, don't ever let me go.

Seven Bridges Road

Words and Music by Stephen T. Young

Drop D tuning:
(low to high) D–A–D–G–B–E

Verse
Moderately

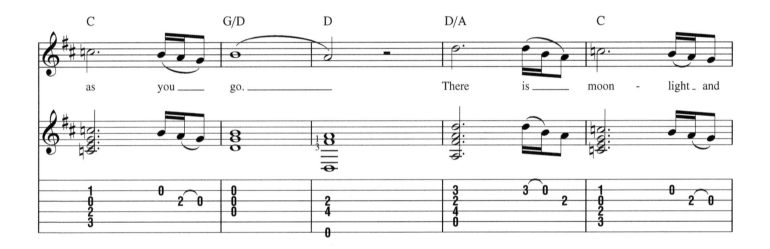

1. There are ___ stars in ___ the south - ern sky, south - ward ___
3. *See additional lyrics*

as you ___ go. ___ There is ___ moon - light ___ and

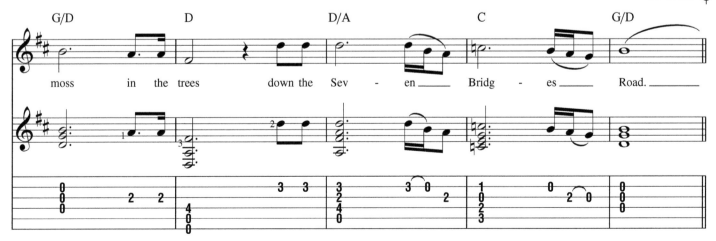

moss in the trees down the Sev - en ___ Bridg - es ___ Road. ___

To Coda ⊕

Interlude

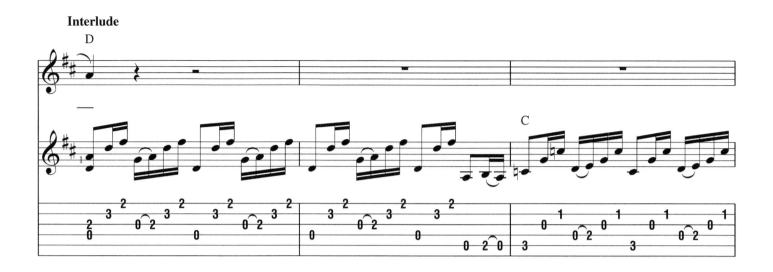

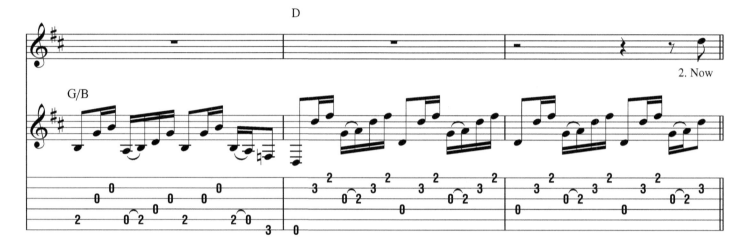

Verse

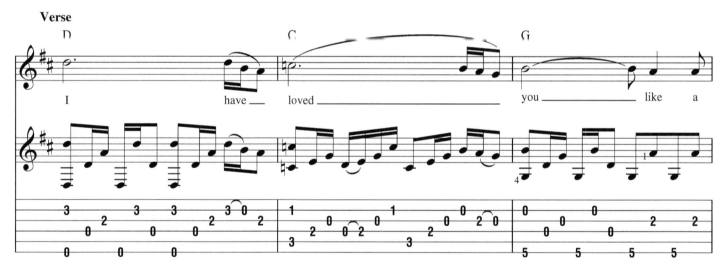

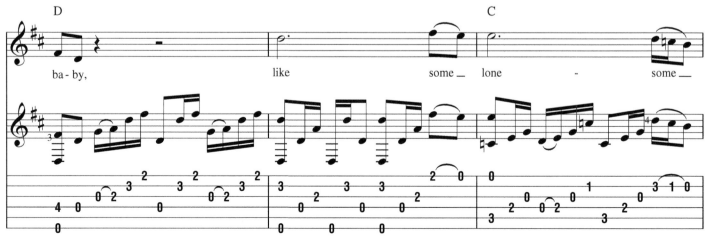

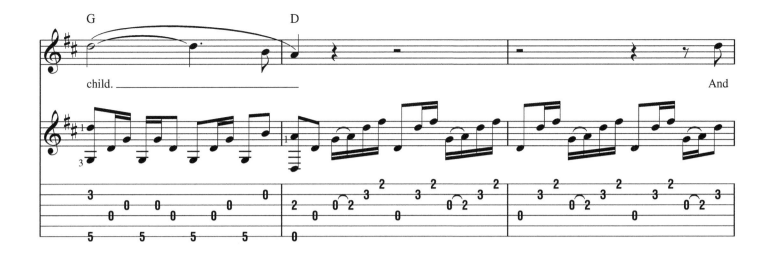

child. _____ And

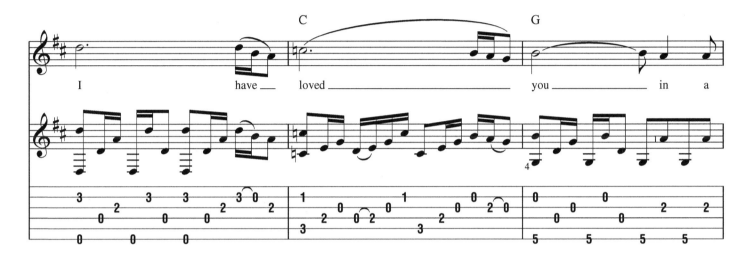

I   have ___ loved _____ you _____ in a

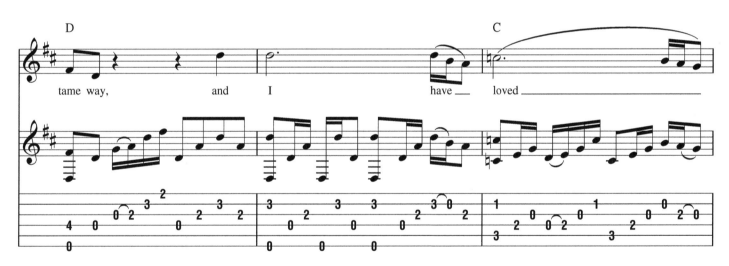

tame way,   and   I   have ___ loved _____

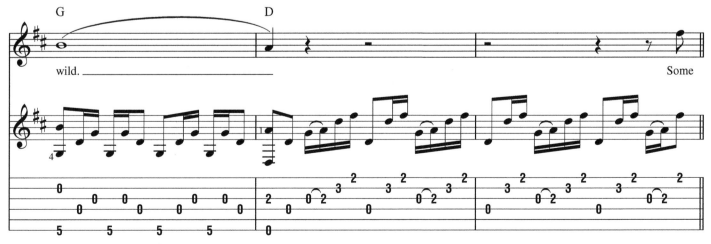

wild. _____ Some

Bridge

times there's _____ a part _____ of

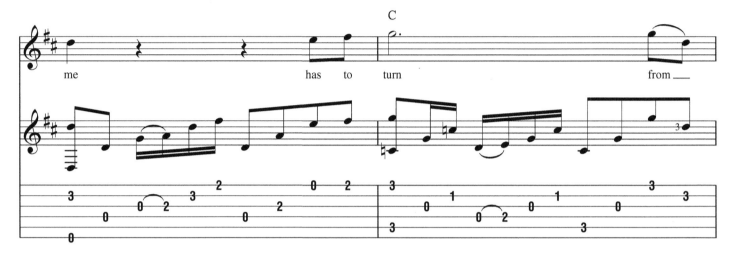

me has to turn from ___

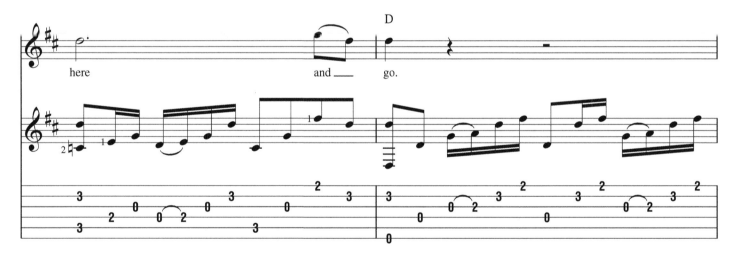

here and ___ go.

Run-nin' like a child from

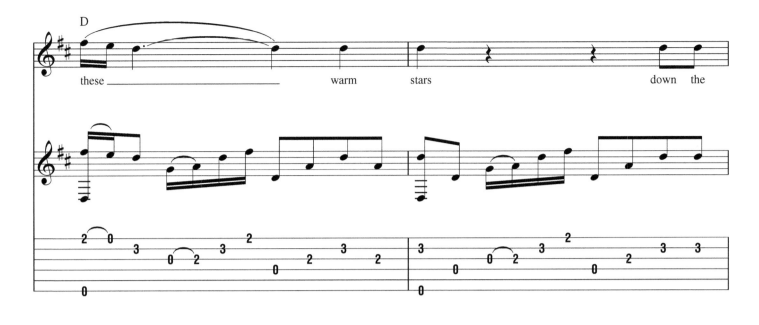

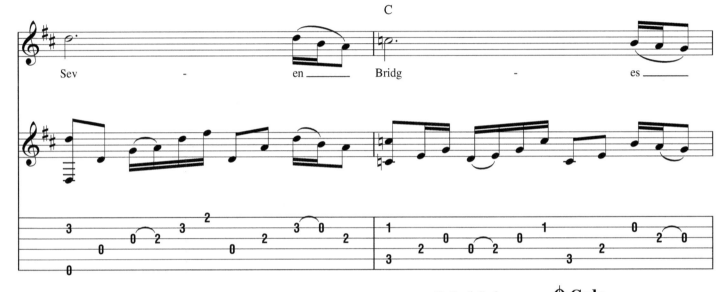

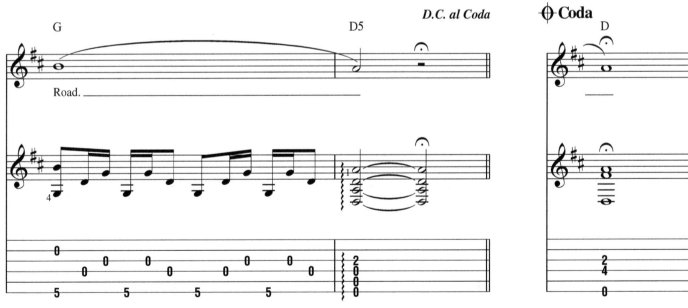

Additional Lyrics

3. There are stars in the southern sky,
   And if ever you decide you should go,
   There is a taste of time sweet and honey
   Down the Seven Bridges Road.

Norwegian Wood
(This Bird Has Flown)
Words and Music by John Lennon and Paul McCartney

Drop D tuning:
(low to high) D-A-D-G-B-E

Verse
Moderately

1. I once had a girl, or should I say she once had me.
3. *Instrumental*

She showed me her room, is-n't it good, Nor-we-gian wood. She
She

Bridge

asked me to stay, and she told me to sit an-y-where, So,
told me she worked in the morn-ing and start-ed to laugh. I

I looked a-round and I no-ticed there was-n't a chair.
told her I did-n't and crawled off to sleep in the bath.

Verse

2. I sat on a rug, bid-ing my time, drink-ing her wine.
4. And when I a-woke I was a-lone, this bird had flown.

We talked un-til two, and then she said, "It's time for bed."
So, I lit a fire, is-n't it good, Nor-we-gian wood.

Outro

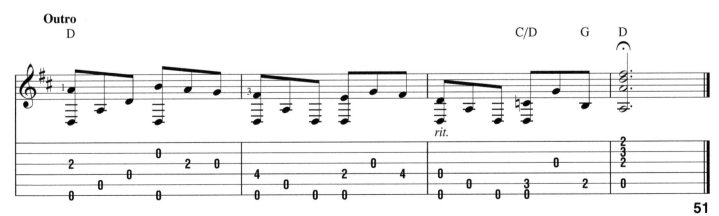

rit.

Wanted Dead or Alive

Words and Music by Jon Bon Jovi and Richie Sambora

Drop D tuning:
(low to high) D–A–D–G–B–E

Intro

Moderately slow

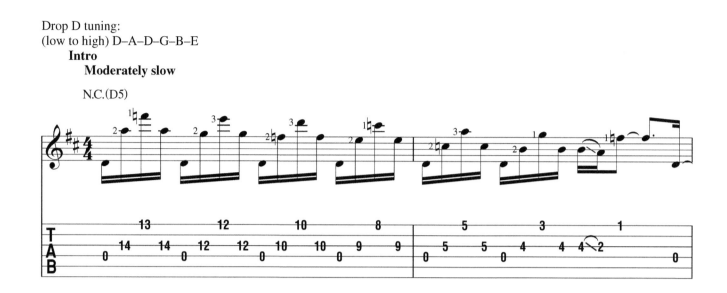

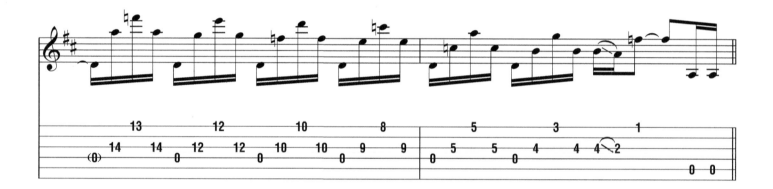

Play 3 times

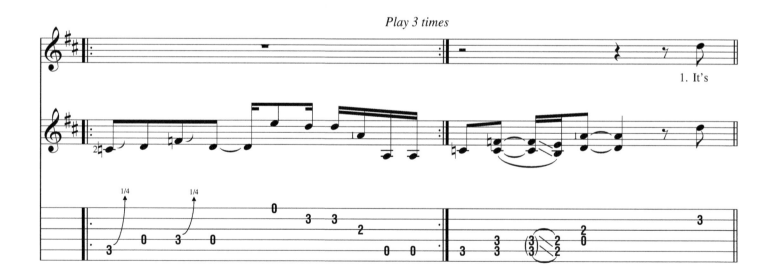

1. It's

% Verse

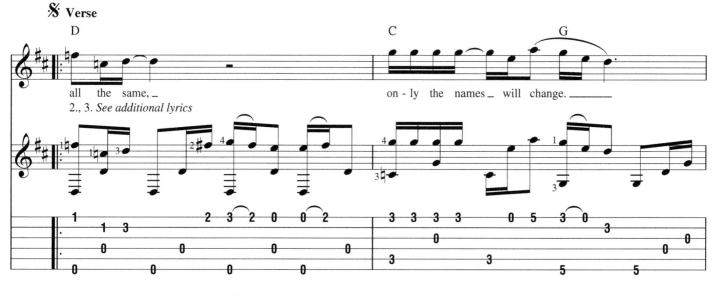

all the same, _ on - ly the names _ will change. _____
2., 3. See additional lyrics

Ev - 'ry day ___ it seems we're wast - ing a - way. ___ An -

oth - er place _ where the fac - es are ___ so cold; I'd

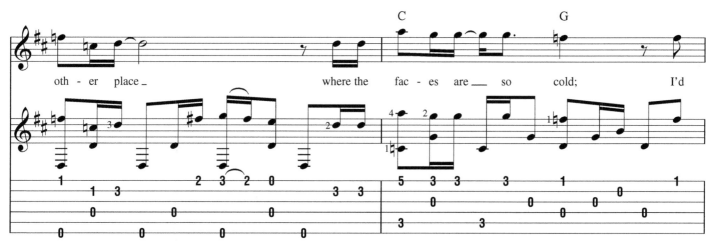

drive all night _____ just to get back ___ home. I'm a

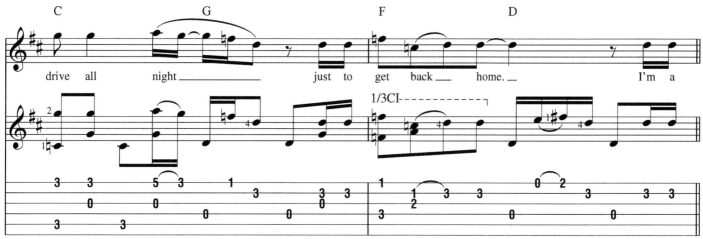

53

Chorus

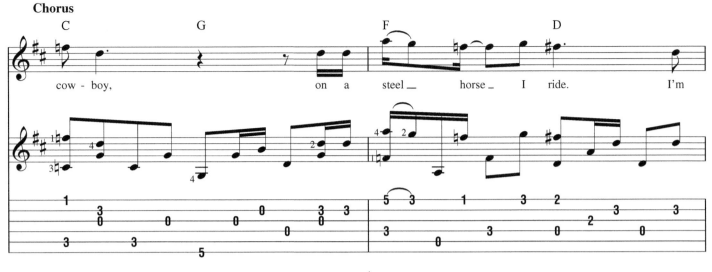

cow - boy,   on a steel __ horse __ I ride.   I'm

To Coda ⊕

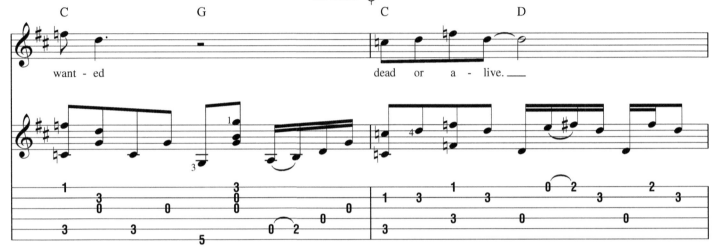

want - ed   dead or a - live. __

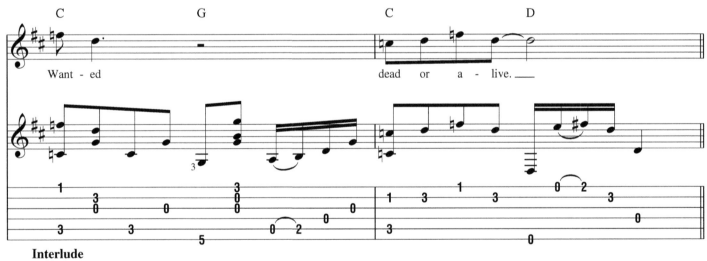

Want - ed   dead or a - live. __

Interlude

N.C.(D5)

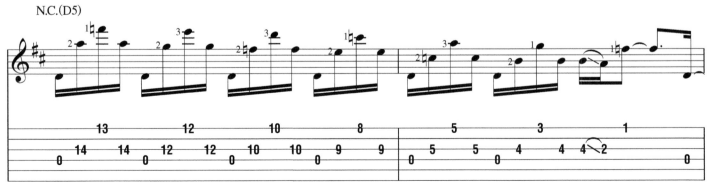

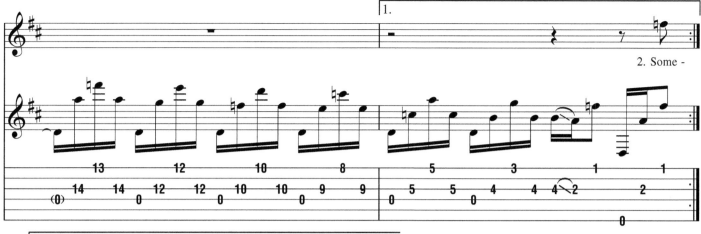

 2. Some -

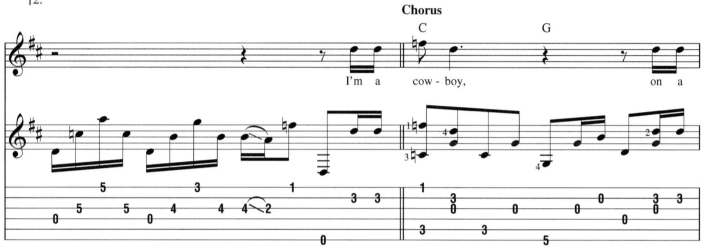

Chorus

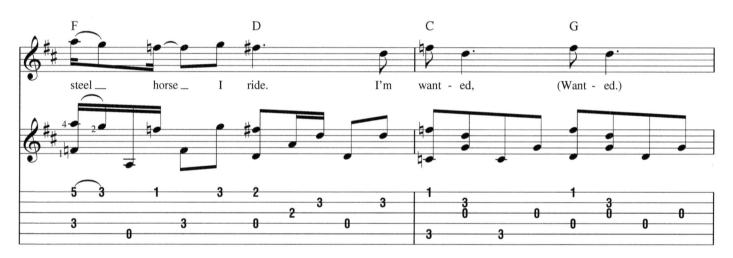

I'm a cow - boy, on a

steel __ horse __ I ride. I'm want - ed, (Want - ed.)

D.S. al Coda   **Coda**

dead or a - live. _____ 3. And I

dead or a - live. __ 'Cause I'm a

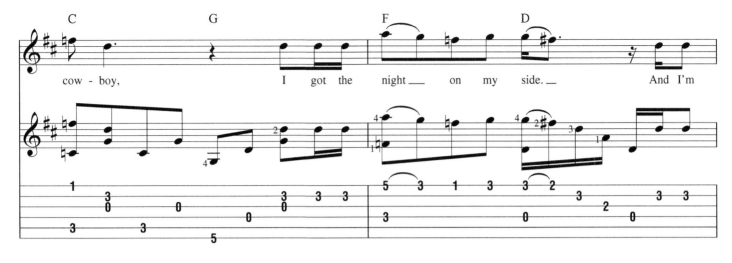

cow - boy, I got the night ___ on my side. ___ And I'm

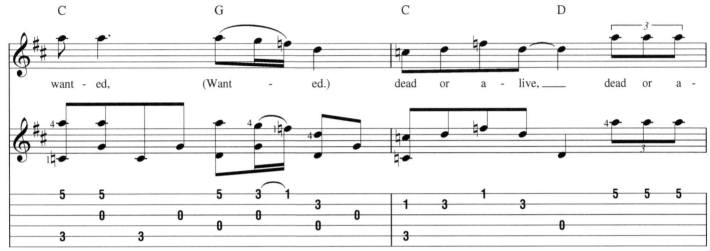

want - ed, (Want - ed.) dead or a - live, ___ dead or a -

live, ___ dead or a - live, ___ dead or a - live. ___ I still

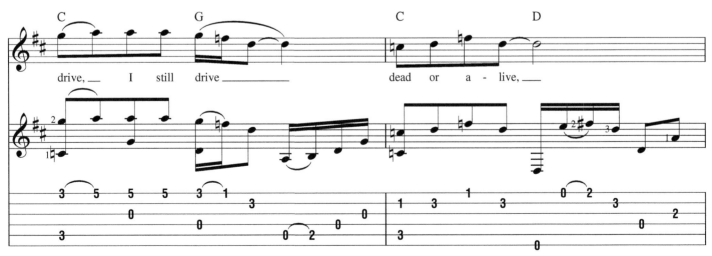

drive, ___ I still drive ___ dead or a - live, ___

Outro

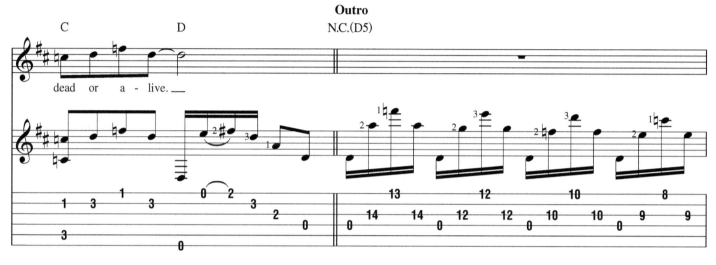

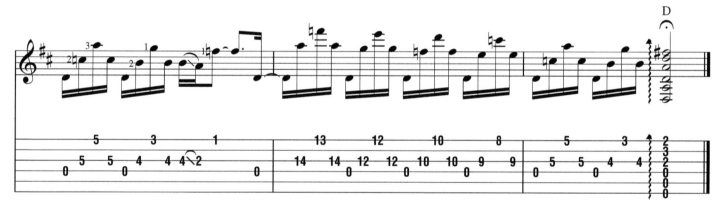

Additional Lyrics

2. Sometimes I sleep, sometimes it's not for days.
   The people I meet always go their sep'rate ways.
   Sometimes you tell the day by the bottle that you drink.
   And times when you're alone, all you do is think.

3. And I walk these streets, a loaded six-string on my back.
   I play for keeps, 'cause I might not make it back.
   I been ev'rywhere, still I'm standing tall.
   I've seen a million faces, and I've rocked them all.

Suite: Judy Blue Eyes

Words and Music by Stephen Stills

Drop D tuning:
(low to high) D–A–D–G–B–E

Intro

Moderately fast

1. It's

Verse

get-ting   to ___ the   point ___   where I'm   no ___   fun   an - y -

2., 4. *See additional lyrics*

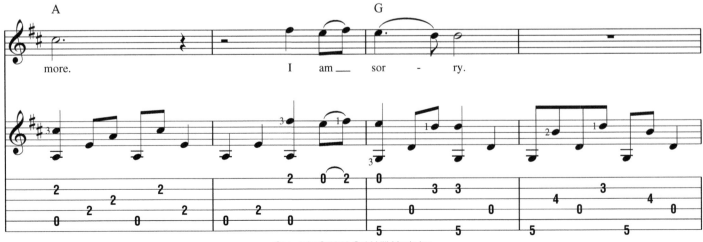

more.   I am ___ sor - ry.

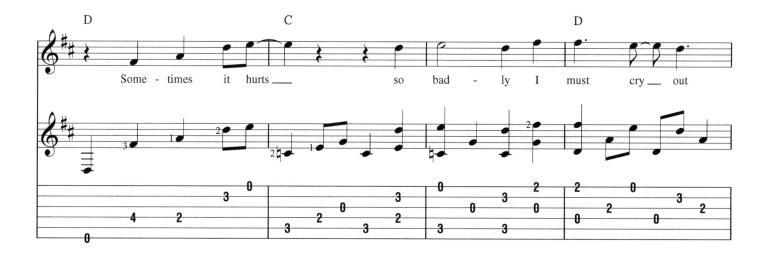

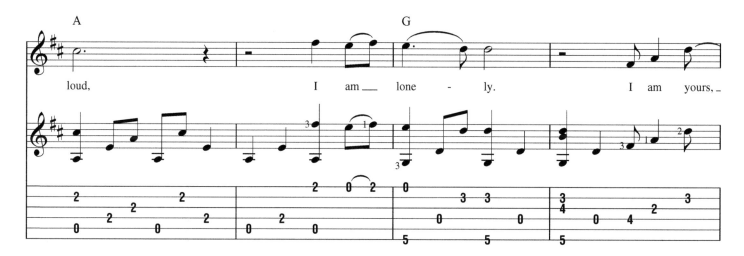

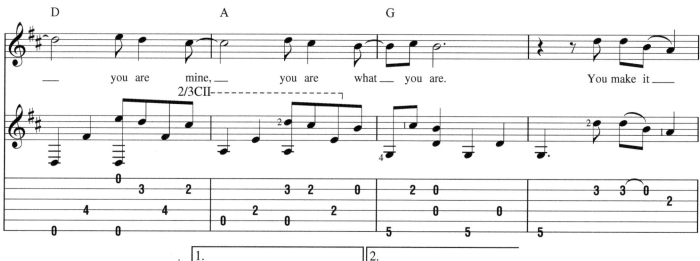

Verse

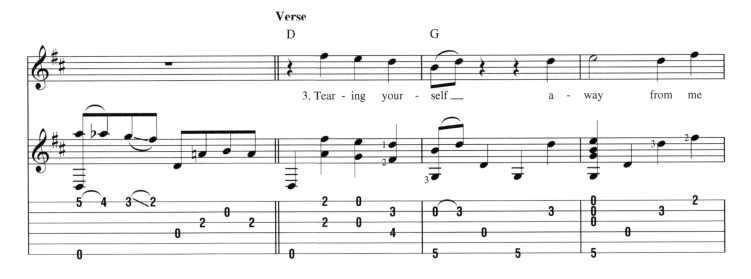

3. Tear - ing your - self __ a - way from me

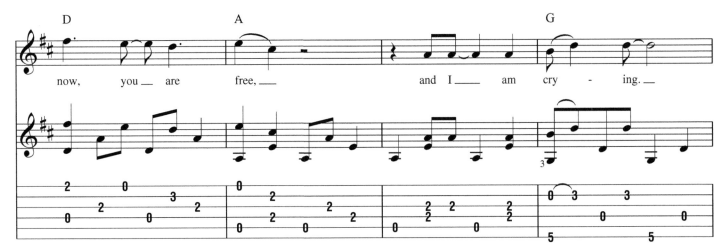

now, you __ are free, __ and I __ am cry - ing. __

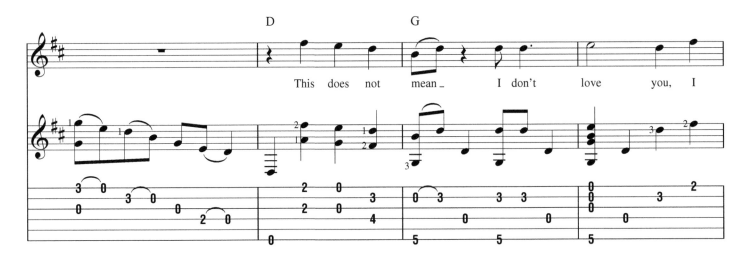

This does not mean __ I don't love you, I

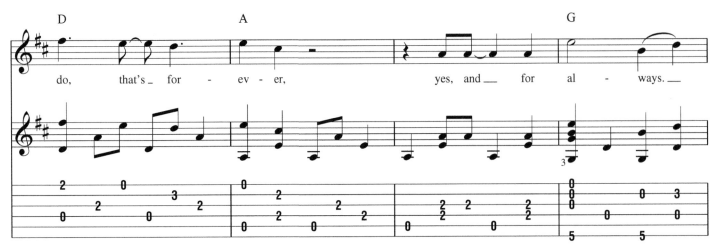

do, that's __ for - ev - er, yes, and __ for al - ways. __

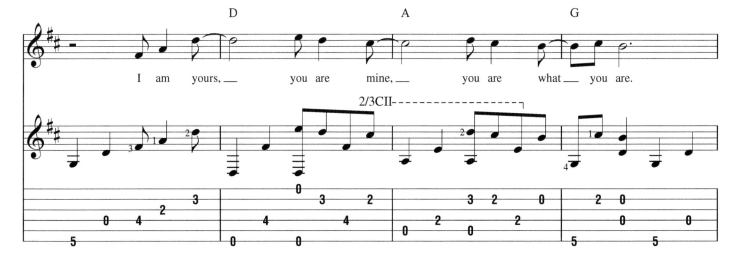

I am yours, __ you are mine, __ you are what __ you are.

D.S. al Coda ⊕ **Coda**

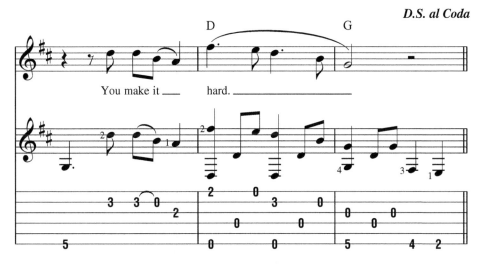

You make it __ hard. _____

__ And you make it __

hard, _____ and you make it __ hard, _____ and you make it __

Interlude
Half-time

hard. _____

Bridge

1. Fri - day eve - ning,   Sun - day in the, af - ter - noon.
2. Tues - day morn - ing,   please __ be gone, I'm tired of you. __
3., 4. *See additional lyrics*

What have you got to lose? __   Can I

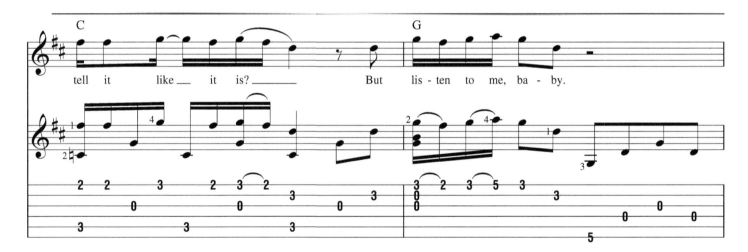

tell it like __ it is? _____ But lis - ten to me, ba - by.

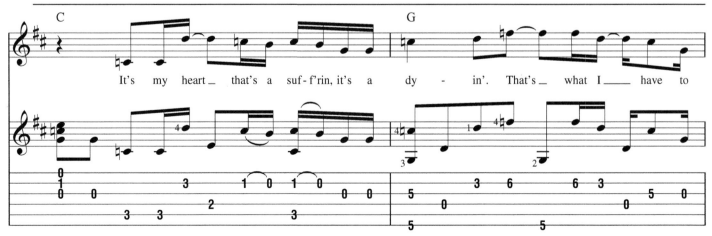

It's my heart __ that's a suf - f'rin, it's a dy - in'. That's __ what I ____ have to

Interlude

Verse

5. Chest-nut brown canar-y,

6., 7. *See additional lyrics*

ru - by throat - ed spar - row, sing a ___ song, don't be ___ long,

Play 3 times

thrill me to ___ the mar - row.

Outro

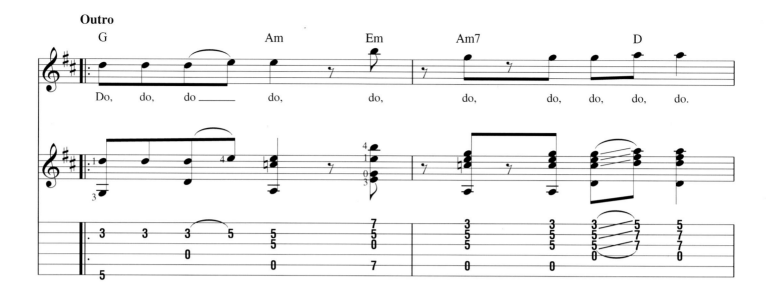

Additional Lyrics

2. Remember what we've said and done and felt about each other.
   Oh babe, have mercy.
   Don't let the past remind us of what we are not now.
   I am not dreaming.
   I am yours, you are mine, you are what you are.
   You make it hard.

4. Something inside is telling me that I've got your secret.
   Are you still list'ning?
   Fear is the lock, and laughter the key to your heart.
   And I love you.
   I am yours, you are mine, you are what you are.
   You make it hard.
   And you make it hard.

Bridge 3. I've got an answer.
   I'm going to fly away.
   What have I got to lose?

Bridge 4. Will you come and see me
   Thursdays and Saturdays?
   What have you got to lose?

6. Voices of the angels,
   Ring around the moonlight,
   Asking me, said she's so free,
   "How can you catch the sparrow?"

7. Lacy, lilting lyric,
   Losing love, lamenting,
   Change my life, make it right,
   Be my lady.